re-entry

re-entry

poems by
Michael White

2005 Winner, Vassar Miller Prize in Poetry

University of North Texas Press
Denton, Texas

10 9 8 7 6 5 4 3 2 1

Permissions:
University of North Texas Press
P.O. Box 311336
Denton, TX 76203-1336

The paper used in this book meets the minimum requirements of the American
National Standard for Permanence of Paper for Printed Library Materials,
z39.48.1984. Binding materials have been chosen for durability.

Library of Congress Cataloging-in-Publication Data

White, Michael, 1956-
Re-entry : poems / by Michael White.
p. cm. -- (Vassar Miller prize in poetry series ; no. 13)
ISBN-13: 978-1-57441-211-6 (pbk. : alk. paper)
ISBN-10: 1-57441-211-6 (pbk. : alk. paper)
I. Title. II. Series.
PS3573.H47445R43 2006
811'.54--dc22
2005030898

Grateful acknowledgments to the following magazines, in which these poems
first appeared:
The Asheville Poetry Review: "cineplex"
The Journal: "beach traffic"; "my bicentennial year"; "mediterranean"
The Kenyon Review: "interim"
The North American Review: "study"
The North Carolina Literary Review: "water street"; "st-paul-de-vence"
The Paris Review: "everything adrift"; "the levee"; "re-entry"
Western Humanities Review: "flood year"; "plat à décor"; "the thicket"

Grateful acknowledgments are especially due to Debbie McGill and the North
Carolina Arts Council, for several grants and fellowships which made this work
possible.

Thanks also to the Vermont Studio Center and to the University of North
Carolina at Wilmington.

re-entry is Number 13 in the Vassar Miller Prize in Poetry Series

Cover image "Landscape with a Farmstead ("Winter Landscape")" by Rembrandt
Harmensz van Rijn is courtesy of the Fogg Museum, Harvard University Art
Museums, bequest of Charles A. Loeser, 1932.368.

for Sophia

contents

one

two

three

one

the levee

I am this dust on the river road, I'd think.
I am this dust on the tasseled fields—deep summer's
scent of brushfire threaded through this breeze—

and at that age, I could believe. My world
consisted of a sallow-looking downtown;
streets named after trees; the girls I worshipped

secretly; the cemeteries fringed
with spikes; the breaks in the river hills to the south
(great floodplain vistas fading away to the south),

where everything ends in a narrow fringe of swampoaks
and cottonwoods overlooming the river . . . Part
of me is always homing, scrambling down

the face of the levee, forcing my way through willows
and driftwood—flotsam of old tires and rusted oildrums—
down to the Corps of Engineers' embankment,

down to the seam where the elements touch, the dense
aortal dark of slaughterhouse and prairie
sweeping past me . . . There at the tip of the wing dike,

kneeling and sinking back, I'd finger the sand grains—
fragments of mussel shells—and let the sun-scaled
body of current carry me away . . .

Sometimes, I'd close my eyes, and in the cries
of crows—the howls of semis two miles off—
in the barely audible, hoarse note of a tractor

raising dust in the fields across the river,
I could hear the year click shut. One evening,
smoldering down to the nub, I thought I could feel

an odd, irregular throbbing in my jawbone—
skull—the balls of my feet . . . The others were back
in the trees: I crouched alone on a spit of sand,

the pulse of an engine pounding all around me,
out of the pores of the limestone cliffsides. Something
was coming towards me, something was churning its way

upriver towards me, thrumming louder and louder
until I could see the train of barges shackled
together—laboring into sight—until

I could see the tow: its funnel pouring gouts
of black exhaust, its pilot house ablaze
with fumes and glare, its six-foot bow wave breaking

along both banks . . . I was amazed, transfixed
by its deliberate and delicate
corrections—centering in its marks—as slowly,

it drew abreast, and I could see the man
inside of it, the one responsible
for all those tons of steel and displaced river.

I remember the eerie, flickering pall
cast up from the instrument panel onto his face,
and I remember the moment he turned towards me,

and sounded his airhorn three long blasts for me
as if in recognition . . . *River rat,*
I thought, and waved. And then he was gone. And after

that agitation passed—long after the gnats
all started up again—I ran as hard
as I could through the flood-washed cottonwoods—over the levee—

back to the road, and my friends . . . In our back yard
today, camellias are having their second spring;
our concrete birdbath fills with the slough of blossom . . .

Suddenly, it's over. Suddenly,
the tendons of clematis flower and fade out
over our garage roof—its metaphor,

its metamorphosis, is over and done with . . .
What I want is what I had: the landscape
beneath the landscape; hawks and cliffheads; hum

of bridges; summer's sumac, gold and cobalt
clarities which deepened as the river
gradually dwindled . . . What I want is what

I was—that self lost utterly in vagrant
days that sank in flames as I spent them there—
my element silt, my posture prayer, my god

appearing sometimes in the guise of gnats
or hawks, or hundreds of incidents that bloomed
alone like bloodlit clouds across the dark

opacities of surface . . . Once, a man
appeared like that, *a man appeared like that*,
and as he passed—as waves of unimaginable

clamor shuddered through that place which still
absorbs me so completely—suddenly,
he glanced at me, and claimed me for his own.

everything adrift

It's less a memory than a darker shade
of feeling that comes back—and less a feeling

than an air of timelessness, the lull
that sets in just before the swell of evening . . .

Luminous cargo, luminous tributaries
sweeping past the plate-glass windows of

the hometown dives where I worked. I'd stand in the front,
in a starched white shirt, and feel the bones of my face

burn up in the cast of sunlight—suspensions of dust—
as the blazing webs of lives belled up like sails

in imperceptible drafts. Sometimes, it seemed
the places themselves were dreams: like dreams which place

the dreamer in a deeply familiar scene,
the low light kindling toward a transitory

equilibrium between the room—
subaqueous, companionable—and

the world, which calls him, calls him, *woos* him, till
the heart forgets why it was clenched in the first place.

That was my favorite hour—that balancing
of the momentary gradients of dusk

like clouded blood in the storefronts across the street,
and everyone inside closed up, dug in, waiting

for darkness and mercy. These nights—shaping myself
to the long scrawl of your body—I remember

feeling the mirror burning at my back,
that sense of everything adrift, as wave

on wave of shadow slid down Eighth St or Ninth St . . .
Twenty years have passed since I peered back down

into that cruciform downtown: its random
suburbs—swerves of river just beyond—

the prairie rising and falling in every direction
as far as one could see . . . Meanwhile, the plane

kept laboring up a sharp incline—dense floes
of cumulus between us and the earth—

as, buffeted by turbulence, we shuddered
and caught ourselves, we shuddered and caught ourselves

—the river's vein of poured lead lit beneath us—
there, not there—then there—then gone for good.

re-entry

Then it hit me. Fumbling for a smoke,
I sank down heavily onto a concrete bench

beside the circle drive. There was no view
except for the rows of glare-shot windshields, shimmer

of asphalt—bypasses and freeways—and
a venomous, blood-orange dusk above it all.

I took a deep drag. Thirty days had passed
since I'd checked in, and wandered through the ward

with torn implosions in each ear—as fireflies
flooded the trelliswork of synapses—

for three straight days, before I knew where I was.
It was the top floor of State Hospital,

our dayroom windows facing out across
the vast exhaustion of the Midwest, where

electrical dust-storms tinged the air, an aura
of migraine settling over the river hills . . .

Day after day, we'd gather there for Peer Group—
some in wheelchairs, some with our IV poles—

each trying to calm the tremors in his hands.
Whenever someone spoke, whenever someone

started to piece a narrative together
out of threads of smoke—the infused ache

of what the flesh remembers—I could feel
the tenor of fear in everything he said,

the word on the tip of his tongue on the tip of my tongue.
I'd listen and gaze out, listen and gaze out over

the fallow prairies, half-imagined hayfields
of my only landscape: buckled faultlines

leveling off in miles of bottomland,
where massive burr oaks loomed like cumulus

adrift upon a plain of dust. I'd stare
and stare—untethered, ravenous—at sheets

of lightning smoldering here and there beneath
a remote steel-blue cloudbank, as the room

filled with acetylene sun, the conduits of
my nerves burned clean . . . And this was the only cure

there was. One day I rose, and put on my street clothes,
nothing in my pockets. I remember

riding the elevator five flights down—
the sudden *whoosh* when its doors opened on

the ground floor . . . Struggling to compose myself,
I strode across the lobby with a wink

for the receptionist, but by the time
I stepped out into the sunlight, I was shaking.

flood year

(in memoriam Penny Austin)

It was a record flood year in that country:
dikes and levees overrun again,
the bottomlands erased as if they had never

been, the minds of burr oaks isolated
on a plain of water. Still, in town,
the streets were merely backed up; evenings brimmed

increasingly fulgent; candelabras of dogwood
lit the outsides of the windows; it
was lovely. I was nearly thirty, washing

dishes full-time—scraping plates through a hole
in the sink all day—but unaccountably happy.
There, in my room on Anthony Street, was a little

fake fireplace—next to the bed—which filled the winter
dark with shadowy shapes of blue. The river,
as I remember, crested twelve feet over

flood stage, held for a week of declarations,
proclamations, then slowly withdrew
from our lives. Or maybe that was another year—

I can't be sure of anything now. Except
that on Tuesday nights, I went to poetry class
with brilliant women I seldom understood.

Our teacher, as it so happened, was Larry Levis:
Larry Levis with his bomber jacket,
Keats-colored gaze, his lanky swimmer's physique

visibly bowed beneath the weight of his second
divorce. He talked half to himself, it seemed,
occasionally slipping sidelong into some story

about the dustbowl San Joaquin farm towns
he'd hated once, but wrote about all his life—
those high school summers staring over the cowl

of his father's ancient John Deere tractor, crawling
between the long vine rows . . . Once, apropos
of nothing, he recited "Skunk Hour" lightly,

effortlessly, as if he'd written it
himself—just finished it, in fact, and needed
to hear how it sounded. As for us, how could

we tell how much of it was him, how much
of it was us, when everything we thought
we knew turned into syntax at its edges,

cadences which made no sense, such loose-leaf
drafts we couldn't fix with white-out. Some nights,
we let out early; some nights, we ran out of things

to say, and simply walked out arm in arm
beneath an avalanche of stars . . . We'd drift,
inevitably, toward the known quantities

of an empty downtown weeknight: reveries
of light splayed downward over the surfaces
of green felt, chalk dust, the decisive thrust

of a cue stick. Maybe we'd split up later; maybe
we'd jumpstart Mia's car again for yet
another late-night Kansas City road trip,

hydroplaning hills of dream, descanting
"Somnambule Ballad" by dome light on
the way home . . . Later, lying alone in my room,

I'd watch the shadowy, delicious wash
of blue flame undulate across the walls;
I'd listen to the periodic crash

of syntax folding over itself. I must
have been tired, but didn't feel tired; I'd mouth the ghosts
of syllables as if they mattered. Fervent

as I was back then, those images—
those lucent sheets of rain transfiguring
the windowpane—were almost enough to live on.

water street

After two hours of pamphlets, diagrams
of right-of-way—the ex-GI instructor,
with his pointer, pointing out how wrong

I was, how wrong I've always been, in fact—
I'm ready to give up. Maybe he's right. It's early
March, Defensive Driving class in a room

straight out of the 60s, with stackable plastic chairs,
steel desks, and too many chalkboards. Most of the students
are teenaged, and dressed to kill—their hair precisely

pressed or curled—except, as it seems, for me.
For me, it's merely a nightmare of starting back
in boot camp, waking on the floor of my life,

but that isn't what concerns me. What concerns me
here, on break—on this side street fire escape
I've found by following the exit signs—

is how the sky is opening, the river
shivers in its skin, its surface film
of blood and oil, as memory ignites

the bridge from this to the other shore. Beneath me—
half on the sidewalk, half in the empty street—
three girls in Levi's and leather jackets cluster,

one of them bending sidelong toward a Zippo's
momentary flame. On days like this,
an acrid stench from the pulp mill miles upriver

stings one's lungs and permeates each pore . . .
These days, the birds won't fly, the flowerbeds don't
disclose themselves, and I can't stay out of my dreams.

But everyone is like that here: these girls,
for instance, preening in Levi's and leather jackets,
one of them flashing her wedding ring—its glancing

flame of diamond. Once, this was a city
with ship-works and rail-yards lining the riverfront,
its sepia dry-docks and Liberty ships all slipped

into oblivion. Sometimes, certain
peculiar details—buttresses or the bones
of wharves—exhume themselves, leach back through the seams

as if from the ocean floor. It took me years
to comprehend, to even register
how the river changes direction every six hours;

how the forests of longleaf pines surrounding us
can't even propagate without being razed;
how everything—rather than moving—simply settles

and rises, settles and rises again. We're still
in shadow, but Memorial Bridge is touched
with an immaterial rust of dusk, the city

incandescing—stone and glass—the moment
I look at it, the moment I close my eyes
in order to fix this scene in mind exactly

as it is. I'm starting to hum a little,
tapping my own gold ring against the rail . . .
Three minutes left till the class resumes, so I screw

the cap of my Snapple back, inhale stray threads
of gossip, smoke—faint guitar chords from around
the block—and I don't miss a thing.

interim

The glass fogged over from outside—
the view how many stories down
to the courtyard where the purple flags

of irises burn through the rain.
There are bedrolls neatly stashed beneath
chairs, black cylindrical ashtrays, pots

of ficus, styrofoam coffee cups;
there are payphones on one wall. Some people
from cities, some people from farms—

but with close resemblances. The double
doors into the ward itself
admit the loved ones only. Here

is the mortal hush, unconsciousness,
and the hiss of respirators. Here
is the body patiently at sea

in its devotion to a mind
somewhere, one feels, somewhere, one feels,
but where? Here is the day which is

not day, the hours of a night which is
not night. Here is the choice which is
no choice, and here is the look in my sister's

eye. Here is the lion of
his will not letting go until,
at last, by increments, it does.

And here is the interim—as one
by one, my brothers and sister slip
away to make their calls . . . Without

really deciding to, I bend
down toward the untouched left side of
his brow. At first, I can't quite reach,

so I roll aside the IV, find
the lever for the safety rail,
which swivels out of the way . . . *No need*

to put things back, I think, as I gently
touch my father's wrist. And here,
at the end of everything, is the kiss.

study

Unseasonable January's
casual revelations—tops
of pine trees limned against a vellum

overcast—redbud saplings sprung up
unremarked, till now, along
the back yard fence lines . . . Reinstalled

beneath the eaves, I'm listening to
the self-delighted shrieks of our fourteen-
month-old daughter, Sophia, ring

through the floorboards over my former study.
I'm not making much headway—
the hour's intentions, intonations,

syllables like insect tracks,
dissolving as soon as I set them down—
but I don't care. I'm happy here,

lord of the loft, eye-level with
the broken crown of our pecan tree,
for instance—swamped where it stands in its sheath

of vines—and the golden swarm of gnats
or of mayflies, hovering above
the pale, two-tone *japonica*

below . . . Such spells hang on for days
sometimes: the atmosphere milk-warm,
our yard unconscious still, except

for this gnat-cloud—swirl of dust—which, hardly
even visible itself,
makes fragrance visible to me,

each scent-drunk spark
of psyche fleeting,
minute, meaningless, but free.

two

my bicentennial year

1. Norfolk. Oceanview Blvd., 1 a.m.

Sick as I was of all the east coast base-towns bleeding
    together in my mind
like one long strip of Oriental saunas, draft-beer
    taverns, sputtering bulbs
that spelled out "E-Z FINANCING," when Eva
    and Carla showed up, nursing

a borrowed Olds—just as they promised—I got in.
    The engine shuddered on its
sheared motor-mounts through every slowdown, hesitation
    there on the edge of the Norfolk
shipyards, but—before long—loped along at 70
    over the jolt of bridge-joints,

ramps, the extinct state roads rocking us out and out
    across the Dismal Swamp's
black reek of sulfur, cypress spoked with moonlight . . .
    Both girls curled abreast the front seat,
muttering in their sleep, a viscous crust of insects
    plastering the windshield.

After three years below decks—breathing steam, forced air,
    exhaust—I wasn't sure
it mattered whether I turned back now or they caught me later.
    What could they do? I wondered;
Why should I care? So six full hours of seaboard passed,
    a little marsh fog in

the headlights, half a pack of menthols, till at first light—
   somewhere in north Georgia—
Eva and Carla slipped out to stretch their limbs, in last night's
   hairdos and halter tops,
and I simply sat there and watched them, letting the truth sink in:
   I'll never go back. If there

was a conscious act that year—the road map spread out over
   the hot hood—it was the moment
we piled back in, all lined up in the front again,
   two perfectly beautiful cocktail
waitresses and one AWOL sailor: nineteen, twenty,
   and twenty-one forever.

After that, what happened, happened effortlessly
   under the white sun of
dry counties, tending a thin beer high between our thighs
   all afternoon, till Carla—
driving—ploughed straight into the back of a seven-car pile-up
   north of Birmingham;

and Eva—riding shotgun—crumpled forward, as
   loose strings of blood flung forward
past my ear, out over the spiderwebbed glass . . . Still,
   we walked away. In fact,
within a few hours, Carla was dancing naked in
   a place called Spot's—a small

crowd riveted to the relaxed, cursive grace of her pelvic
   thrusts—and I woke up
to a clatter of trays in county jail the next day . . . But
   let's skip that. Skip ahead
a few days, to another state, where the pine woods subside
   gradually down and down

to canebrake and fencerows over black furrows of delta.
    Then we were barreling flat out
westward—specters of oil rigs rising in the distance—
    stretches of powerlines sagged
with blackbirds constantly beside us . . . Then we were crossing
    the Lake Charles bridge, where the Olds

shook loose its tailpipe, belched dense showers of sparks the rest
    of the way to a sidewalk café
deep in the Quarter, where we never laid eyes on it
    again. For this was New Orleans,
city of human scale—the body keening *touch me,*
    touch—the river of rivers

two blocks off. *We're here,* we thought, rum coke in our mouths.
    The Quarter then was set-piece
Dixieland, with disco/drag bars mixed in—absinthe
    cut with silicone—
and sucked us in completely. Both girls disappeared
    into an underworld

I'd only see in glimpses—mis-takes—afterhours
    clubs crammed with lounge-acts, various
stages of pre-op and post-op hustlers feeding off
    each other . . . As for me,
I vanished differently—in plain sight—wearing a chaste
    red blazer and bow-tie, packing

a roll of fives and ones (with a fifty wrapped around it)
    pressed against the inside
of my thigh. I was the one you trusted—you
    among the throngs on Bourbon—
I was the one who'd keep an eye out, serve your watery
    cocktails, and take your money.

How I felt burned—clarified—by that city. Almost
    as in the *Purgatorio:*
in that moment Dante and Virgil cast themselves
    through the scourge of flame—the earthly
paradise just beyond—the sentinel angel singing
    "Beati Mundo Corde"

straight into their ears . . . And though, as it happens, I
    was technically a felon,
somehow I didn't think of it quite like that. That
    was another world, I thought,
while in this one, I stood on the corner of Bourbon and Conti,
    barking at the top

of my lungs: *no cover charge,* to anyone—no one—over
    the wrought-iron balustrades
of evening. August, then September passed: the wreathing
    depths of the river mists
slid into the Vieux Carré for good, as the tourists ebbed
    more slowly toward some music

in their heads. And what I heard was, Carla was gone;
    I never saw her again.
But Eva would come round—Eva still came round every few nights—
    all leather-booted and laced-up,
hipbones narrow as a boy's. As one feels weather in
    a wound, or divines water

beneath stone, I'd sense her coming long before
    I could actually see her:
parting the waves of tourists, tresses flung back on
    the blood rush of her beauty.
Once, in a borrowed apartment—crucified in slats
    of moonlight—we made love

as tenderly as children, all night, till the night's
    last chords of zydeco rasped
and died off somewhere beyond Canal. I couldn't believe
    how lucky I was. In time,
when we slept, we slept uncovered, dreaming a common dream
    of sleeping outside, a heavy

snowfall sifting down upon us . . . Still, we kept
    warm—pressing ourselves together
where we lay—and slept on into the storm. And once,
    when I woke, I watched her sleep
for a long time, taking such shallow breaths; I studied the faint
    white lines, distensions of

childbirth across her breasts and stomach. That's when I noticed
    the faded tracks and washed-out
veins of her wrists and forearms . . . And all I wanted then
    was to trace each wound with my lips—
but just as I knelt, she curled in her sleep, and by the time
    I woke again, she was gone.

2. Detroit

Fastforward now to Warren, Michigan: industrial
    lake winds lacerating

my wrong clothes and thinned-out blood where I stood on
    Coolidge or Packard, Studebaker or

Konszai . . . *Just give me two weeks to kick it,* she'd said. And now
    here I was, my pockets filled

with tip change, greasy curls on my collar. Here I was stalking
    the methadone clinics, Cyrillic

shopfronts and one-way glass of everywhere she'd been.
    Her sister's house, for instance:

a faded bungalow, all but invisible in the leafless,
    workaday emptiness . . .

I hovered close enough to hear the resonance—
    the hum inside of it—

but never entered the yard. Instead, I followed my ear
    to the end of Ten Mile Rd.,

where I crossed a great embankment, shimmied a gap between spans
    of chainlink, straddled the guardrail—

easy as that—and stuck my thumb out into the howl
    of I-75 southbound.

I remember standing stock-still on a gravel shoulder—
    sights set on a little

town, a friend out West—and though I nearly froze
        before the first car stopped,

soon one thing led to another, and to another . . . And so,
        without much effort on

my part, an undercurrent carried me across
        the Upper Midwest: Alton,

East St. Louis, the moonlit K.C. railyards . . . After
        a while, I slept, and felt

the flexures of the Flint Hills rolling like oceanic
        crests beneath my wheels

until I opened my eyes in Denver. Have you ever
        been in one of those big rigs

wailing through its gears—its upper registers
        of being—before it finally

reaches speed and smoothes out? Almost immediately,
        I'd nod and slip off into

abyssal dreams—and no one even seemed to care
        if I rode for days in silence,

unaware of anything much except for the wipers
        cycling back and forth

across the caul of sight. On I-25, one night,
        a trucker handed me

a lit joint—then a thermos spiked with bourbon—feeling
        starting to filter back into

my limbs again . . . *Sweet Jesus*, I said, giving in.
    A thousand miles had passed—

another thousand yet of onramps, broken glass,
    the rest stops of amnesia

turning to air behind me . . . West of Laramie
    was desert winter—windblown,

ice-blind—and whatever buoyancy or grace
    had carried me across

the continent so far was gone. The truth is, thousands
    of us were working the freeways

that year—looking for a way out—burned-out scarecrows
    you wouldn't dare pick up.

Thank God for that last ride with a Nez Perce mill-hand, about
    my age, in a battered ranch truck,

tracing the dorsal curvature of Idaho
    through the mid-December dusk.

We rattled along; rain turned to snow, then back again;
    great banks of storm-scud backed up

over the blue, serrate spurs of the Sawtooth ridge,
    then swept across the boulder-

broken slopes of pine—loose wisps of aspen—meadows
    grazed to barrenness . . .

Good luck, he said, when he dropped me off. I spent the night
    on my feet beneath a concrete

overpass—peering out through a whorl of snowfall—stamping
    down hard to stir the blood,

each bone a blue ache gradually going numb. At first
    I thought of Eva—curled

on the car seat next to me that night, as I let long drags
    of cigarette smoke stream sidelong

into the rush of wind . . . And for a while, my mind
    kept flipping through these random

images of the road: stray riffs of music—half-
    remembered farm towns—water

towers and silos glimpsed from the interstate, like little
    shipwrecks riding out

the rolling swells of the Kansas dark . . . But mainly,
    I was concentrating

all night: willing every last iota, spark
    of energy into

a tiny point of blue flame—like a pilot light—
    still needling on at the exact,

empty center of my ribcage. Suddenly,
    a door in the sky slid open—

vast andromedas of fire bore down on me
    as the temperature bottomed out.

What could I do, when spasms of shuddering took hold—even
    my peacoat frozen through—

and I didn't think I would make it? What could I do but cleave tight—
    shifting my weight from side

to side—my gaze a slit which took in the starry blaze
    outside? . . . What happened was

I managed to hang on till dawn spread—by grain and iceglint—
    over the floor of the gorge,

then floundered back out the same way I'd come—through the
    waist-deep drifts which covered the road—the firs

and lodgepoles all around me moaning beneath their loads
    of snow. What happened was

I labored out through the canyon mouth—out into a brutal,
    wind-shorn plain I couldn't

remember seeing before. The road was already ploughed—
    the valley perfectly treeless,

perfectly featureless, except for the towering, uniform,
    vaguely angelic shapes

of electrical pylons filing across the emptiness—
    a low vibrato of

high-tension wires drawn taut from here to there. A feeble
    sun came up. By now

I was headed north through reservation country, gathering
    strength the farther I went.

Sometimes, I wondered: *What is this dream I am walking out of?*
    Sometimes, I thought I could hear

something, and stopped, and turned . . . But it was nothing, it
  was always no one. Thirty

or forty miles to the east, the abrupt spine of the Bitterroot
  Range was rising in

a milky light; and above that, long contrails trailed
  through an otherwise cloudless sky .

three

mid-air

Evening clamps down sharply earlier now—
as if beneath the press of a thumb—as I wend
my way through a parking lot, and look for my car.

Another autumn's panoplies have streamed
away, like one continuous scattering
of rapture, every moment sliding out of

mind, to sea . . . But there is a sky which does not
change—beneath which an old friend, Michelle
and I, walked through our newly renovated

campus, past its wrought-iron bridges and benches,
beds of utterly yolk-gold black-eyed Susans,
artificial hills and artificial

ponds, with full-grown willows and cattails, all
of it shining in its best light then, that night
of the famous poet's visit. Free for the moment,

we had fifteen minutes for coffee (I
was telling all my favorite stories about M.),
when I saw something sidelong which startled me.

Two workers were digging neck-deep in a hole—
one white, one black—and in that instant (sole
of my foot suspended in mid-air), I remembered

the scene in Dante's hell, where Ugolino—
frozen deep in a pit of ice—seems bound
by fate, by the logic of that place, to gnaw

the nape of his enemy's skull—himself compelled
to stand and suffer there forever. Still,
these men, the two I saw that day, were merely

digging their way down to some sewer line,
or water main, maybe—one of them bent
in profile, his brow splattered with mud—as we passed,

coming to the end of the anecdote
beneath a livid dusk. I blurted, "Hey man,
you better wipe your face," the sole of my foot

a few inches from the earth as he froze and turned
to look at me—eyes widening visibly,
as if in disbelief . . . He was light-complected,

neither black nor white, as it turned out,
but plainly—plaintively—stricken, childishly whispering:
"*How could you say that? How could you say that to me?*"

and in that numbness, that stunned lapse, it dawned
on me that he'd been horribly burned somehow—
his brow a mask of purplish scars drawn taut

around his lashless eyes. He looked at me:
that part of the face which momentarily brims
with gusts and shades of feeling, normally—

for you or me—swept vacant, affectless,
reflecting nothing. I could see his pupils
dilating in sun the moment he took me

in; and I think I raised both hands palm outward,
making myself say, "Sorry, man. I didn't
know." But the truth is, we never missed a stride.

The truth is, we didn't dwell on it, and went
back a different way. The only way out of Dante's
hell is deeper and deeper down, it seems—

the poets descending Lucifer's hip, until
they reach the core of the earth, where they writhe completely
upside down, then haul themselves up headfirst

into a cave of stars. He thought the fires
of purgatory burn away what's left
of one's life . . . I wish I could believe that. I

was talking about the ends of days, the mind
laid open by such incommensurate wealth—
until the stoplights change, and the traffic crawls

away . . . But there is a sky which does not change:
its signatures of cirrus half dissolved;
its starlings stopped in mid-air, mid-impulse;

its sun fixed blazing furiously above
the library forever. I suspect
I'll take into the next world, and the next,

the memory of his childlike cry—as he turned
to face whoever spoke—that one who saw through
everything about me I can't live with.

mediterranean

I'm lying on the beach at La Napoule—
    the lion-colored Îles
de Lérins hovering on the seam between

two intense shades of blue. It's a balmy, lucid
    April afternoon.
Three days ago, a ship materialized

offshore—an immense, solitary, gray
    American aircraft carrier—
and I couldn't help wondering, *what is it doing here?*

Since then, I've seen them everywhere I've looked,
    it seems: young sailors drifting
awkwardly, in twos or threes, among

the bars and kiosks lining the Croisette.
    And I've spent some time reliving—
reconstructing—how it felt to cross

the North Atlantic below decks. The truth
    is that I didn't really
believe in much, except for the ship, my job,

itself—the lit fires, heat and shattering din
    of the engineroom itself—
as it loped along forever at seventeen, eighteen

knots across the waste and wrack of dream.
    Month after month, I'd simply
hang on for the hour we'd anchor *here*,

for instance—or somewhere a lot like here—with these graceful,
    white or blue archaic
fishing boats, called *pointus,* sheltered behind

the seawall; with these equally archaic
    bollards spaced beside
the quay; and looming above it all—above

these cream and apricot-tinged terraces—
    the peaks of the Alps themselves.
It's one of the essential situations—

states of mind—this sudden waking, stone
    by stone, my paycheck cashed,
my fingernails scrubbed with Ajax. Maybe it doesn't

seem like much, and maybe it isn't. But
    in 1975,
there were no wars to speak of. "Exercises,"

or "drills," maybe, but nothing romantic, nothing
    heroic happened. Still,
it's what I had: a couple of hours of freedom,

wandering the dregs of the waterfronts
    in Palma, Villefranche, Naples . . .
Napoli, as I remember it,

consisted of a million souls of Fiats
    tearing themselves apart
beneath a sulphurous, purgatorial pall.

Night after night, I'd ride the liberty launch
    to its berth beside the vast
marina's carapace of glass and rust—

and step into the Piazza del Plebiscito's
    open space of fountains,
opera, ossuary, statues of eyeless

martyrs, saints and virgins of a gutted
    church. Night after night,
I'd wander off into that instant dissolve—

weightlessness—where nothing is what it seemed
    to be, like the patently
illusive auras of amazons who hung

around fleet landing in stiletto heels,
    their haloes real. Medieval
labyrinths of alleys, balconies

of laundry, everyone out for an evening stroll
    in this city which knows me—city
which sees me as I am—each footfall, brush

of a fingertip, each flick of a cigarette ash
    or a glance. Whenever I passed
the chapels of Sansevero, Gesù Nuovo,

Santa Chiari's stanzas of ochre stone,
    I wanted to slip inside
an air the mind could still itself for once in:

some inverted, half-imagined hull-shape
    filling in around me
till, my eyesight used to the dim aquarium

light, I'd kneel and confess everything . . .
    Somehow, I never did;
I'm not sure why I didn't. But I recall

an overlook on San Martino—hundreds
    of feet above the roofs
of the burnt-out slums—with unimpeded views

of Campania in every direction: the Isle of Capri,
    and the dusky, inauspicious
profile of Vesuvius across

the bay. I'd stand there, light up, stare at the intricate,
    porous passageways
of hell; angelic orders of palazzos;

spot-lit liquor billboards. Most of those evenings,
    opening like a flower
around me, ended badly. All I had

was solitude, a soul which loved to climb
    and look back at the world,
a little money to burn. One night, a man

in a dove-gray, tailored suit approached me and said,
    "You look like Perry Como."
I remember a carnival of ships:

the inexpressibly sylphlike Sixth Fleet frigates,
    tankers, tenders, even
one Soviet sub in dry-dock there below.

And then the stranger standing next to me—
    this short, impeccably groomed
and olive-complected man—leaned over and flashed

some shiny, foil-wrapped object half concealed
    in his hands. It's easy now
to see why trouble haunted me: one part

of my nature drawn out of itself, across
    incantatory azure
distances; another part already

reaching for whatever happens to be there.
    There, in the rush of wind
and blood, I could already taste the heart of the rock

of the proffered Lebanese hashish . . . Even if I
    said nothing—staring at
the strand of pearl-white beacons outlining

the great volcano set against an iris-
    tinted evening—even
if I said nothing, and turned away. Last week,

the train I was riding shunted into La Bocca
    for repairs; and since
I had no choice, I hopped a guard rail, crossed

the corniche road, and walked the beach five miles
    through scripts of spray—the driven
seethe and wallop of waves—to the chateau.

How fortunate it felt, how utterly
    my element . . . Today,
it's Sunday. Here on the beach at La Napoule,

there's something about the luminosity—
    each lit swell breaking at
the last instant upon these pebbles of black

basalt; about this clear, cool sunlight, burning
	without sensation—which stuns us,
all of us beachgoers, inch by serene inch.

This cliff for a headboard, feet aiming vaguely seaward:
	none of us comprehends
 the plots of the books we've brought. On my last day

in France, I wanted to write about restlessness;
	I wanted to write about coming
back in the middle of one's life—that sort

of thing. Sometimes, I think I can feel the ache
	of granite steps in my legs,
the ordinary fantasies of the hour

pierced with the periodic syntax of
	the poem I held out for.
Sometimes, I wonder whether I tell these fables

to myself in order to misremember
	loneliness as bliss,
the deep distractions of that interim self

as partial ecstasies—the only kind
	available for who
and for what I was, it seems. Whose ears could scan

sub-audible engine resonance; whose eyes
	could distinguish the immaterial
smudges of islands through heavy fog; whose nose

could intuit the currencies of paradise alley
	anywhere we'd land . . .
And yet who had no clue. This sand is *soft*.

I love to bury my hands in it; I love
    to spread my arms like Christ.
I've never felt so comfortable in my life.

I realize I'm starting to cave beneath
    the cumulative weight of waves,
but now and then—between the murmurs, yelps,

loose threads of conversations——*there*: the tremor,
    tone of sibilance
I've listened to for two months . . . For a while,

I listen harder. Then I let it go.

plat à décor

Whatever my expectations coming here—
past the rusting palms of the Place de Gaulle, the gates
and ramparts of the Vielle Ville—all I see,

in the foyer of Château Grimaldi, the
Musée Picasso, is a couple of plates:
four heavy, rectangular terra cotta platters,

each with a bird (a pigeon, owl or dove)
engraved upon it. It's the weight, the sheer
ordinariness of earthenware we love

but take for granted. These are ordinary,
too, in just that way: each outline traced
with a fingertip; glazed with the hues, the actual

blue-enameled dazzle of Antibes.
Upstairs, among the paintings I have come
here for—*La Joie de Vivre, Antipolis,*

Ulysses and the Sirens—there are plates
in every corner and passageway, obsessive
studies of women or fauns. Still other plates

are merely things (like the sequences of fish,
for instance—the soles, sea urchins and moray eels—
some with a sprig of parsley beside them) which seem

to complete the whole. But I haven't learned that yet.
I'm backed up against the wall, to let a group
of children through—their pants' cuffs rolled, their sweaters

knotted around their waists. They file past, stepping
carefully, and glance about—as if
expecting to see the master himself, bald as

Prospero, rise from a sawhorse table. All
I want at this moment is to follow them—
to trail along with the slowest child—the tour guide

starting to lecture now in a tongue I can't
quite keep up with . . . It was 1946,
she says. Françoise was pregnant, Paris was spared.

And since the war—the years from *Guernica*
to *Charnel House*—was done, he came here, where
the sea remembered him, his landscapes lit

with the airily childlike faces of its gods.
He was sixty-five, and learning a different art:
he didn't have time to finish anything.

But it's the rush, the accidents, the reckless
smudges of splattered slip we can't resist.
These children filing upstairs—hand in hand

with each other—understand. I think I know
what it felt like, filling in the empty space
with memories like a spume of stars, each image

studiously unschooled, which—in its glaze
of gold or azure—says, "There's more than enough
for everyone here. Come in, and help yourself."

st-paul-de-vence

I remember the Tintoretto in the nave—
St. Catherine glowering through a votive haze—
and just outside, next to the Romanesque tower,

one great palm crowning the epicenter of
the perfect *village perché*. City of god,
one seamless exudation of the upthrust

mind of stone; forked lightning of mimosa
blossoming through the valleys miles below.
This wasn't ten years ago, it was last week:

the moment I stepped back into that lick of sun,
where the only direction was down through a *frisson* of
medieval alleys, Renaissance staircases

which stumble and catch, which stumble and catch themselves
in vaults, arcades of weightlessness, and bijou
rooftop gardens. But the truth is, something

didn't feel right. I remember wondering why
La Place de la Grande Fontaine didn't reek of piss
or of fried sardines; and I didn't need to see

another pot of bougainvillea, not
another "atelier" with monochrome landscapes
on display. And I was already gone;

I had already reached the gates of the Porte Royale
when the pang of a midwestern diphthong caught my ear.
It was merely a couple of teenaged girls on tour—

one auburn, one dark blonde—relaxing there
on the machicolated ramparts, hundreds of feet above
the vineyard hillsides. After a month abroad,

it was nothing in particular; it was
the voice I missed. The blonde was reclined on her elbows,
one of her ankles propped on the other knee,

her plump calf framing a perfect V of sky . . .
I couldn't help noticing how the ache in each cell
of her sixteen-year-old body, splitting against

its will—each clearly articulated leaf-tip
pushing out—was figured in the delicate
pencil-line of fuzz traced from the cleft

of her navel, down and beneath the snap of her cut-offs.
Meanwhile, her friend was rambling on, while rocking
back and forth on her palms—as if about

to slip off the edge of a swimming pool or a dock.
"How many seconds do you think it would take?—I mean,
you might lose consciousness, black out before

you hit the ground," she said, as she stretched one long
and sandaled foot *en pointe* into the wind . . .
"But what if you just gave in?" she added,

"what if you simply gave in to
the ecstasy, the rush of freefall?
Think of the *thrill* you'd feel!"

beach traffic

It's bumper to bumper now on Market Street,
where rank upon rank of billboards crowd in close
above new growths of stripmalls and filling stations—

each with its sealed-in, stone-faced attendant.
So much of our lives, we focus straight
ahead, into the glare afflicting us—

its waves of white coronal heat igniting
windshields/mirrors/sunglasses, as if
we were never here. How can we help but fasten

ourselves to stray braids of cirrus, vast
flotillas of cumulus that drift across
the mind of sky? How can we help but wander?

We know nothing will bring back that lost state:
house we built with our hands; that host we held
so delicately in our mouths; that blue

we wanted to wade out through, in some other life
we don't recall. I'm humming a little song
beneath the lyres of power lines crossing at

right angles hundreds of feet above me . . . *Dunkin
Donuts*, *Hooters*, and *Coastal Pawn*; the great
flamingo reefs afire; our bodies less

material than the heat fumes billowing
like wraiths without end, robes of angels out of
the sheer dissolve of asphalt, glass and of sheet steel.

Girders through the tree tops. *Future home of.*
(Nothingness.) Our ordinary hours
of solitude, of patience or impatience.

I'm afraid the correspondence I once
sought—that resonance of image, emblem
of the soul—was only a childish dream.

I'm idling a few cars back from the intersection,
feathering the clutch by reflex—in sync
with the brakelights just ahead—as a file

of cars on my right pulls out for the left turn toward me,
each accelerating as it turns,
some cutting it close, some veering a little wide,

and I'm thinking now how a gust of leaves can skitter
past, sometimes, so lightly I hardly notice.
—Sometimes, I'm thinking, all I notice *is*

the void, the absence after. Faces blurred
and affectless, distracted or simply bored,
roll past. I stare into each one: each seems

a few steps ahead, or else behind themselves.
Then the last one; then the last one after that.
I'm probably late. This brand of sun on the back

of my neck . . . and then, swept forward as the moment
breaks (all eye/hand, ball of my foot depressed),
I drive into the void, the absence after.

the thicket

As after a death—I haven't moved a thing—
hemmed in by silence, lathe-and-plaster. What
is lost is not here, not elsewhere, and yet

I wander warily among these hues,
this furniture she chose, as if it were. These
blistered and water-spotted ceilings. Rows

of the white, hexagonal, porcelain bathroom tiles
buckling so slowly no foot notices,
and the kitchen linoleum—left from the 60s—cracked

along tectonic planes. I'm safe, at least,
I tell myself. But the songs that used to wash
through my mind—melodic lines, the rewound scripts

of abjectly reverent love—are gone. And in
their place is nothing: winter ghosting among
the inkstroke outlines of oaktrees, solitude.

And then, today, the weather cleared—the fog
all finally burnt away—and so, when I stepped out,
into the disembodied air, I simply

stood on the porch, and marveled at how mournful
last year's beach toys looked; how the mortar was crumbling
out from between each brick in the fascia; how

the dense, unkillable ivy had returned
on the north side of the house. I traced one seam
in the brickwork—powdery sandgrains clinging to

my fingertip—then drifted round, past the beds
of the dead camellias, each shrub threaded through
with a rusted snarl of wild bamboo. (I remembered

digging for hours one day, pickaxing down
through the rocky loam, till I finally gave up, knelt,
and tore each rhizome out by its root, that spread

so inextricably through the darkness there—
in the lee of the house—like the tentacles of dream.)
I didn't even go out back, but I

could see enough of it—how masses of
wisteria had slung itself like laundry
through the trees, the delicate canopies

of dogwood and pecan laboring beneath vines
as thick as the ropes I once climbed in gym class. Here
was the whole yard crumbling away, the ground half sand,

half oystershell—which I'd flung back uphill
each April, shovelful by shovelful.
I might've opened the gate onto the concrete

patio we used one Sunday evening,
once, in our first spring, its state of being
almost perfectly unlooked-at, almost

perfectly complete. And next to that,
the little, rock-ringed, hyacinth-and-birdbath
island there—at the center of it all—

dissolved beneath the lineaments of weeds.
I didn't move. I stared at the outside of
the house, where our five years of summer sand

and kisses clogged the drains, and then behind—
where what had come of my midlife was a kind
of marshy thicket, all it was evidently

meant to be. Let the major and minor keys
of the floorboards warp as they want, I thought; let the coiling
and pendant vines—tendrilous smilax and greenbriar—

link up over the shed roof; let the breaking
surf of ivy claim this thicket for
itself. I tried, I thought. I couldn't save it.

cineplex
(for Maria Eugênia)

I have a painter friend in São Paulo
    who can't walk past a church
without at least stopping inside for a moment.

This was in Menton, several years ago:
    we were coming down the hill—
half-hurrying to catch the regional train—

her light gait over the stones ahead of me
    all day, the alleyways
cascading down turn after turn to sea.

By the time I noticed the nondescript graystone
    cathedral next to a park,
Maria had already gone in. Then,

when I followed—into the operatic, whale-ribbed
    gloom—I didn't even
glance around, for I was marveling how

she could be—simply, quietly *be*—in such
    a place, her fingertips
splayed lightly on the back of a pew, the aim

of her attention hovering like a question
    mark unanswered there
—like candlesmoke above the altar. What

I thought was that she took in what was offered,
    and no more; but she
was already gone (out through the other door).

     *   *   *

I have always loved the winter forest—any
    winter forest—its
clean, gestural, charcoal hatchwork limbs describing

what?: dependencies of latitude,
    of weather, vascular reach?
—I think of the roughed-out clarity of Rembrandt's

Winter Landscape: how a few, quick strokes
    evoke the thatched roofs of
his polderlands, like a shorthand scrawl of love . . .

Last night, at the cineplex, the face of an actress
    beamed down through a hole
in the back of our skulls, her luminous smile suspended

thirty feet above me where I crouched.
    When it was over—even
though I'd started to weep, as I sometimes do,

each unexpected, misplaced gust of feeling
    spooling out of me—still,
by the time I'd re-emerged into the cold,

the whole thing dissolved utterly from mind.
    As I drew the first breath, clutched
my jacket, crossed the windswept parking lot

—the night pines all black ghostly sway above
    the neighborhood surround—
I had a strange sensation I could feel

the deep insuck of waters, hundreds of miles
    of estuary just
beyond the city limits. This was the moment,

midstride, I remembered entering
        another vast cathedral—
top of my head torn off—that singing feeling

I'd come back to a place I had never been
        before. I must have been eighteen
and not yet born—sun splayed majestically

through tiers and undergrowth of stone. Side-chapels—
        each in its own orbit—
glanced into disinterestedly, in that

slow flowering-forth of compass points. This happened
        in Palma de Majorca;
Franco was still alive. I thought, and still

think there was something in the manner space
        was apprehended there—
where light poured through such perpendiculars

of weightless stone—which dropped me to my knees
        in time, with an overwhelming
urge to pray . . . but I didn't know the right words

to say, so I traced one thumb down the front of my brow,
        and memorized it all.
This never happened to me again. The dead

are dead for me now. But with the same cold shock,
        another memory,
another hour came back: the other side

of the river, down the heart of the cypresses
        and slash pine barrens of
Town Creek. And not simply what took place, what

I saw, came back, but everything: black trunks
    which rise on manifold knees;
the undulant rafts of waterlilies; sweep

of teablack constancy, that threshing wind;
    that roof of burning clouds.
This was last week, last Sunday afternoon,

and the occasional, startling splash ahead—
    some heavy-bellied fishstrike,
maybe an alligator's tail-flick—felt

like a revelation. —Even though it was only
    half an hour spent paddling,
drifting, half aware, upon a surface

so opaque, the tips of my fingers vanished
    if I happened to let them
slip beneath it . . . After a while, I let

the kayak cartwheel aimlessly downstream—
    the weight of my body simply
cast off as my soul, my cinema

had narrowed to a slit, which registered
    the individual droplets
clinging to each blade-tip . . . Suddenly,

I was soaring in great swoops above the miles
    of blonde lacustrine marshlands
fanning out as far as I could see;

and then, I was peering down upon the squat,
    industrial, rust-and-concrete
riverfront of the town where I live; and then,

almost as suddenly, I'd come back down
    again to real time, sweeping
languorously along that falling tide

to sea. Of course, it wasn't anything
    like being born on your knees
in Spain, with all sensation's curvature—

its equilibrium of leaded cobalt—
    kindling in a blast
of luminosity, which shuddered through me—

through my skin, though it didn't even seem then
    like my skin, but felt
more like the skin of sentience itself

stripped back and parted then—each nerve exposed
    for the first time to the burn
of oxygen . . . It wasn't anything

like that, but it was *something*—it was nothing
    more than consciousness,
which swirls each instant constantly out of

our ken—"sweet nothing," as a poet once wrote, this

those women

Turning in midair, I'm clowning back
at her where she stands in her new pink Ariel
swimsuit. *All the time in the world*, I'm thinking,

grasping my knees as I clench myself, and tuck
against the pristine blue—a perfect salvo
shooting up above me in that moment

after I punch through. But then—as I
begin to breast stroke straight up toward the surface—
suddenly, an image of myself

comes back to me. I'm seven years old. I'm pissing
against a tree on Broadway, after school.
It was a two-lane street then: picket fences,

women with beehives driving their station wagons
slowly past me. Pale green sycamores
of freshest April; infinite minarets

of cloud; yet what was in my head a total
blank. —Maybe I thought they couldn't see me;
maybe I wasn't sure I even existed

in their world. —Or else I didn't think,
but simply *knew* particularities
of neighborhood dog barks, root-hove sidewalk jolts

transmitted through my bike tires most of my life.
Now, in a kind of sleepy, resigned love,
I'm settling down at the pool's edge, thinking: *farewell*

to the real, concreteness, all the body's
certainties grown distant as those women
who drove past me every afternoon—

candescing in their canopies of flame—
each cresting the hill in her turn toward the suburbs,
anywhere, the only way out of here.

santa croce

I've stopped for a moment, holding a paper bag
with a carton of milk for Sophia in it, and another carton
of blood-orange juice for Sara and myself. Also

a second, smaller bag, with a couple of flaky *crema*
from the corner. Dante's shadow stretches halfway
across the piazza—bright light on the opposite

façades. The statue itself—this massive, nineteenth century
civic monument on the parvis next to me—
has a haggard air I'm starting to warm up to: the poet's

book slung low in his right hand; wrapping great folds of robe
more tightly around himself with his left. He's glowering off—
his deep-set, visionary gaze aimed vaguely over

the hieroglyphic, *Quattrocento* frescoes of
the Palazzo dell'Antello, over the towers of
the Bargallo and the Palazzo Vecchio, into

the cypress hills beyond. There's no one out yet, except
pigeons on the stones, the tinny wail of scooters
piloted by hundreds of teenaged girls, mostly—

who ride full throttle, rattling their tailpipes over the worn,
black granite heart of the *centro*. Awkwardly, I step back
as an elderly Franciscan friar sweeps past

—his long white vestments and rope belt trailing behind him—and,
in the space of an instant, I can see an ordinary
envelope in his hand, bearing a name—one word—on it,

in a generous, looping cursive I can almost read.
I want to get back to our room, but I'm content for now
admiring the spirally shapes of the wrought-iron streetlamps filing

down the sides of the square—slab benches, emptiness . . .
And into this semi-lucid semi-dream, the first
tour group arrives, their faces a little pasty in

the sun, their tour guide holding a folded compact umbrella
forth like liberty. They might be Germans, Brits
or Americans—all roughly the same age, same color hair—

as they gather milling about beneath me, gazing up at the poet
("Well, he sure *looks* like he's seen hell," one woman says),
then at the geometric, neo-Medieval, green-and-white

Carrara façade, which took so many centuries,
I've learned, to get around to. Shops are starting to open
on the ground floor: postcards and film and T-shirts, scarves

and gold and Murano glassware. Satchels and posters, leather
jackets. Glancing off the surface—half seen, half
translated—nothing to hold on to, except for this heft

in my right hand, this pure weightlessness in my left . . . Almost
in spite of myself, hour after hour I'll come back to
this scene like this; I'll write whatever I see in my Marble

Composition Book: the vendors fanning themselves
behind cardboard displays of faux designer shades
—so many pairs of mirrored irises staring back.

At noon, young couples lunch wherever they can—on
the next bench over, for instance—as I write: "his mussed-up
academic look," or "the fluent bronze-green depths

of her eyes" by which she holds his attention as she harps
about something—maybe a sister, maybe a friend
who frustrates her. I might be fooling myself, but I

believe I'm seeing them in some privileged light they can't
perceive themselves because they're *in* it; some innate,
quick consciousness at play in the way she keeps one eye

on him, as she tips her body carefully back, in order
to take the sun more deeply in through the medium of
her face, her skin—in order to make this offering,

now, of everything she is. —That's how it seems,
at least, to me. Meanwhile, the day unspools as one
long pulse of light as, stone by stone, the sweet, hypnotic,

mostly illusory old world we aspire to asks:
what are you willing to overlook for paradise?
Across the piazza now, I've stopped to circle the little,

nameless, marble fountain there—its lionhead spigots,
basins shaped like halfshells—looking intently, till
I notice somebody crouching behind it, rinsing her arms

in the lowest shelf of water. Quickly, I look away—
as if I had never seen her bathing here, in the middle
of Via Verdi, using the tail of her long, black skirt

as a washrag. Maybe, I think, she's homeless; maybe she's simply
an exchange student, far from home. I'll never know;
in any case, I've already walked away. I'm starting

to realize now how the city has halted all around me:
everything breathes a breathlessly intoned prayer or curse . . .
Which is about when I connect the numbers of

tricolor flags which decorate balconies and blank walls
everywhere, with this surge of oceanic tension—cafes
overspilling the street—which draws me in, along

with the rest, to peer at the portable set above the bar:
the players sprawled like lovers in the green, green grass.
It's 3 p.m., the moment South Korea defeats

Italy, 3–2—and the air goes out of every
lung. As for myself, I'm already following
the parabolic weariness of Via Neri

back toward the basilica. I'd wanted to see
the west light pouring in through the great Venetian rose
above; I'd wanted to see the intricately inlaid

trusswork of the barn-style roof I've read about.
But, lying propped in the Door of the Prophets—her gaze
    washed out
by the direct light—it's the woman from the fountain (who,

as I see this time, is homeless). In the Polaroid
of herself she holds, she's standing next to a boy—her son—
on a clean, white bed, in hospital. And suddenly,

I have to look away again. Emblazoned over
the main door—at the base of the lunette—a gilt
inscription reads: O CRUX AVE SPES UNICA.

And then I step across her—casually step across
her leg—in order to enter this inheritance
of *gravitas* and leaded light . . . A few yards along the right

is Michelangelo's tomb; and then, a little farther,
Donatello's tabernacle: Mary rising
to her feet—alarmed, astonished—half turned toward

the angel, half away. Then Giotto's frescoes. Bodies
like passing thoughts—some whispering to each other, others
praying as best they can in the roped-off section of pews.

And once again a voice begins, in a rumbling, intoned
register addressing no one. I don't know
how long it is before I step back outside, circle

back, and drop two euros into the woman's cup.
This is the hour the city takes stock of itself,
when watchtowers and belfries take on a spectral shine beneath

the straw-gold aftermath of day. The vendors have vanished.
Next to the fountain now, a teenaged couple has stopped
in their tracks to kiss. They're almost absurdly beautiful—

lost in themselves—each cupping the other's face in their hands.
I'm trying not to stare, but at this hour, it seems,
these lovers are everywhere. Maybe they're killing time,

or maybe they are what time itself is: each lover
in locked embrace—ecstatic and alone—along
the wide stone ledges of the *lungarno,* up against

the warmth of bridge rail, park bench, lamp post, anything . . .
For nothing else exists nor can exist for them
within the knots of these hour-long kisses, in this in-

finitesimal tenderness of touch which dissolves traffic,
throngs of tourists filing out of the galleries
—the charter buses trundling them away—even

the Duomo itself, its immense cupola mindful,
seashell-like, at the center of it all . . . It's true,
I think: they're *everywhere,* while only a handful of spires

still catch the last light, only a few stray angels still
gaze down on us, their serene faces half erased,
as if by acidic winds. I've walked out midway over

the Ponte alle Grazie for the moment—motionless
sheets of dark glass sliding past, the steady purl
of current slipping over some spillway I can't see.

I'm staring straight down into the paneled water, at
the cloudy, dislocated image of a door
which hovers there—a few feet beneath the surface—sunlight

seeping around its edges. Hundreds or even thousands
of walkers have all turned home by now; a very old couple
passes close behind me, holding hands and dreaming—

I want to say—of crossing bridges, holding hands.
All day I have walked in a haze of anonymity,
but now this light, its deep descending gradients,

has all but drained away . . . When I look down, the door
I've imagined opens as if by itself, and there, in the hall—
in a wash of undulance—is Sara smiling, Sara

holding Sophia (both in their pj's), waiting for me.
How many steps, I wonder, would it be from here
to the Borgo Santa Croce if I *run*, four flights

of stone stairs turning to air beneath me? I arrive
a little out of breath; the room smells of espresso
and sunlight. Sara praises the pastries I have brought.

We sit, we tear them apart. It's the first day of our lives.